WineNotes

a place to note your wine discoveries

JULIE TUCKER
JENNIFER ELIAS

SMARTS CO

SmartsCo creates fun, stylish products designed to give you essential and intriguing information about some of life's greatest pleasures—wine, food, sex, chocolate, coffee, beer and more—all in a memorable way. If you want to learn more about our other products, visit our website at www.smartsco.com

SMARTS^{co}

WineNotes by Julie Tucker and Jennifer Elias

© SmartsCo 2003, 2005

Published in the United States by SmartsCo
530 Howard Street, #450
San Francisco, California 94105

ISBN 0-9721876-1-8
2nd Edition, Revised 2005
10 9 8 7 6 5 4 3

Edited by: Ray Johnson
Design: René Huber

Printed in China.

table of contents

Welcome to WineNotes, a place to review, rank, and remember what you drank. Fill this notebook with your thoughts, observations and of course the occasional wine stain. While you're at it, you'll enhance your winetasting skills with every entry.

WineNotes is designed for wine lovers of all kinds, from the wine novice to the seasoned enophile. Here you'll find many essential facts of wine, from regions and grapes to the correct pronunciation of words like "Gerwürztraminer." Putting everything you need to know between the same covers.

Enjoy!
Jen and Julie

We met over a glass of wine in the Spring of 2002 and realized that we share a similar approach to wine– enthusiasm for exploring new tastes, the pleasure of sharing wine with friends, and a desire to learn much more.

We wanted to create a way to learn about wine that was fun, not dry or full of snobbery. So we created WineSmarts—the question and answer cards the make learning about wine as much fun as it is to sip. WineSmarts has found an enthusiastic audience, including star chef Mario Batali, *Food & Wine*, *The New York Times*, and much more. We then joined up again with wine educator Ray Johnson to create this little WineNotes book to keep track of all the wines you taste.

We're now busy creating other ways to explore life's greatest pleasures, including wine, food, chocolate, sex, beer, coffee, and more.

sniff

The tasting experience is as much about smelling as it is about tasting. Your senses of smell and taste are closely intertwined, so taking the time to sniff a glass of wine will add to your tasting experience. You'll find that some wines have layered aromas where one aroma is strong at first, and another a few minutes later. The aroma and taste may go together or may seem completely unrelated.

To bring out the aromas in a wine, swirl it in your glass.

Though it may seem a little silly at first to swirl, it actually "opens up" the wine—that's winespeak for letting in air—and helps you experience the aromas. Fill your glass about one–third of the way, so you can swirl without spilling. Then, go ahead, swirl it around, and take a sniff. What does it smell like? Do you like it? Swirl and sniff again. Is it the same? Or has it changed?

Aromas may be as diverse as blackberry jam and wet cardboard, vanilla and cedar. Smell is also a very personal thing. One person may detect cherries where you note pineapples. There's no correct answer—it's more about exploring the range of aromas and sharing your discoveries to help you define what you like.

sip

Now, taste the wine. Hold it in your mouth for a moment. How does the taste compare with the smell? Is it what you expected? How would you describe it? If you're having a hard time putting words to wine, here are some common terms for describing wine:

These words are part of the standard wine vocabulary, but don't worry—you don't have to memorize them. Use whichever words best describe what you taste and smell: barnyard, zucchini, cherry candy, cream soda, dirt, etc. Your own personal wine "code" will help you remember the wines you've tried and what is similar or different about them.

FRUITY
A lot of rich, fresh fruit flavors like blackberries, cherries, pineapples or peaches.

ACIDIC
Acidic wine is usually described as "tart" or "crisp." Too much acid can make a sip of wine feel like sucking on a lemon, but too little will make the wine taste flat and dull.

TANNIC
Tannins generally produce a puckery taste, not unlike that of an over-steeped tea. Tannins add structure to red wines so the taste doesn't slip away in your mouth. Tannins are a naturally-occurring part of wine that come mainly from the seeds, stems and skins of the grapes.

HOT
We're not talking sexy here. This is a wine that tastes like it has a lot of alcohol. It can actually make your mouth feel a little warm.

BUTTERY
Taste a little butter in there? That's a common flavor that comes from a process called malolactic fermentation. The winemaker puts the wine through an additional fermentation that converts malic acid (which has a crisp, apple-like taste) to lactic acid, which is softer. A byproduct of this conversion is the smell and taste of butter.

OAKY
Many wines are aged in oak barrels, which can give the wine a range of flavors and aromas, including caramel, butterscotch, and oak wood. Those oak barrels are expensive, so some wineries take the cheap route and dip a bag of oak chips in the wine, to give it that richer flavor.

BODY
Body generally refers to the structure of the wine and describes how heavy and substantial the wine feels in the mouth. It can range from a light, crisp Riesling to a rich, smooth Syrah.

BALANCED
This is how a wine's fruit, alcohol, acid, tannins, and other aspects relate to one another. When one component doesn't overwhelm the others, the wine is considered balanced.

FINISH
This is the taste that stays in your mouth after you have sipped the wine. Does it last a long time? Or does it disappear?

spit (Yes, spit)

While it may not be pretty, spitting can actually help keep your palate "fresh" if you're tasting a lot of wines. It also helps prevent you from getting so inebriated that any glass of wine tastes great to you. You can use a small disposable cup and spit subtly. If you're having a wine-tasting party, it's always good to supply some cups in case people are planning to drive home.

and scribble

Now that you've tasted the wine and
explored the aromas and tastes, use
the tasting sections and note your
experiences. Use a few key words, some
symbols, or whole sentences—whatever
works best for you. Then try the wine
again, perhaps with some food. Has the
taste of the wine changed? Jot that down
as well. This will help sharpen your
winetasting skills.

how to use
WineNotes

Record your wine discoveries with information about wine grapes, regions, vintages, wineries, and some sensory triggers to help you remember the wine —when you tasted it, with whom, and what you might have eaten with it.

There's plenty of space to take notes on the wines you taste, beginning on page 52. The notes are separated into four categories: red, white, sparkling, and dessert. As you'll see from the example, there's no right or wrong way to take wine notes. We've simplified traditional "tasting sheets" so that taking notes on your wine discoveries is quick and useful—helping you refine your palate, and keep track of wines you've enjoyed (or not) and why.

winery __Chateau WineSmarts__   vintage __2000__

region __california dry creek__

grape(s) __zinfandel__

color/aroma __deep, inky color/smells of spices & green pepper__

taste __cooked jam with some herbs and cinnamon thrown in__

overall opinion __2/11/2007- tried with David, Chris and__

__Wendy w/ hamburgers. Next time try w/ BBQ'd ribs.__   price

★★★ Yum. $10

Here's a quick summary of characteristics of the most common types of grapes.

You'll find that certain grapes produce distinctive flavors and aromas. These become more obvious when you taste them alongside wines made from other grapes. But be prepared for exceptions. A Sauvignon Blanc might taste like many Chardonnays you've enjoyed. Or, you might encounter a Cabernet Sauvignon that seems like a Merlot.

Even the most expert wine tasters are sometimes fooled. A famous example is the story of wine experts given a glass of red wine to taste—they described it with a range of typical red wine descriptors—only to discover that it was a Chardonnay dyed red!

what's in a Year?

Have you ever wondered why everyone is always talking about vintages? Every year, wine magazines, books, and guides proclaim the best regions of the vintage year and many people keep vintage charts or try to memorize this information.

The vintage is the year the grapes were harvested—no matter when the wine was bottled or released. But is it really so important?

Well, we may go out on a limb by saying this, but we don't place much importance on the vintage as an indicator of a wine's quality. There are more interesting—and useful—things to remember. Sure, there have been great growing seasons when the weather was perfect, the grapes were ripe, and the heavens parted. Yet vintage charts all too often obliterate the fact that some winemakers make terrible wines in good years and others make excellent wines in bad years. After all, many variables beyond soil and weather factor into a wine's quality.

Many factors influence each wine, from grape types, region, weather, and winemaker, to your mood, the wine's age, and the foods you're drinking it with. It's not an exact science by any means. Some of these characteristics may not sound appetizing, such as the cat pee characteristic common in many Sauvignon Blancs, but somehow when in wine, it works.

grapes + characteristics

whites	grapes	characteristics
	Chardonnay	pear, apple, tropical fruits
	Gewürztraminer	rose water, lychee, perfume
	Marsanne	herbaceous and full-bodied with some floral notes
	Muscat	orange blossoms
	Pinot Gris/Pinot Grigio	crisp, candied fruit, minerals
	Riesling	floral, peaches, limes and kerosene
	Roussanne	aromatic and acidic
	Sauvignon Blanc	high acid, citrus, gooseberry, sometimes even cat pee!
	Sémillon	rich with some pineapple
	Viognier	perfumey, peaches, apricot

grapes +	characteristics
Barbera	ripe currant, smoky
Cabernet Franc	a greener shade of Cabernet Sauvignon; green peppers, vegetal notes
Cabernet Sauvignon	full-bodied, tannic, cocoa, black currants, tobacco
Grenache	fruity, low tannins, higher alcohol
Merlot	smooth, plummy
Mourvèdre	dark, fruity, fully structured
Nebbiolo	licorice, tannic, powerful
Petite Syrah	deep-colored, inky, tannic
Pinot Noir	cherries, raspberries, earthiness
Sangiovese	earthy, lightly colored, lively acidity
Syrah	black fruits, tar, meaty flavors, black pepper
Zinfandel	berries, jam, spicy with black pepper

reds

a few words on
Wine + Food

Do you enjoy toothpaste with orange juice? Probably not. How about warm chocolate chip cookies with ice cold milk? Now, there's a classic combination that most people agree on.

With wine, there are some similar classic food and wine pairings. But just as some people hate milk with everything, you may decide you don't like those pairings either. Let your taste buds make their own rules.

Foods can change how a wine tastes in dramatic ways. While there are some classics, such as Cabernet and leg of lamb, there are also many others such as champagne and potato chips that work well.

A general tip is either to pair wines and foods that share an aspect such as acidity, body, and sweetness, or to intentionally choose wines that contrast with the food so the differences are enhanced.

For example, acidic foods such as tomatoes often go well with more acidic white wines such as Sauvignon Blanc or Pinot Grigio, or with a red such as Chianti (an Italian wine made from Sangiovese grapes). And richer dishes, such as crab cakes in a white butter sauce often go well with richer wines, such as a buttery Chardonnay. If you want to create contrasting flavors, try pairing a pasta in a cream sauce with a more acidic wine such as a Pinot Grigio that will cut through the fattiness of the dish.

Another general guide is that foods high in protein, such as red meats, can mellow out a wine with a lot of tannin (that tea-like, puckery taste you may get from some red wines). So a steak or leg of lamb may go well with a Cabernet Sauvignon or a Syrah.

Some wines are more versatile than others and, in the end, you may prefer rich red wines with fish or a white wine with your burger. Taste and see.

Wines are made throughout the world,

from Alaska to New Zealand and from Hawaii to Slovenia. Different regions often produce wines that are distinctive because of the soil, weather, and local winemaking practices. Some regions are particularly suited to growing certain grapes. Bordeaux in France and Napa in California both have warm summers that create good growing conditions for Cabernet Sauvignon. Alsace, in France and Germany, and the Anderson Valley in California have cooler temperatures that produce good Riesling.

Familiarizing yourself with wines from different regions will both expand your palate and help you recognize how a variety of regions create different kinds of wines.

Some European countries have very strict laws regarding which grapes can be grown where, and how the wine is produced—France and Italy in particular. On the other hand, the laws of countries such as Australia and the United States are quite lenient.

Throughout Europe you'll also find official wine and vineyard classifications and ranking systems like *Grand Cru, Premier Cru, Qualitätswein, Tafelwein*, and acronyms like DOCG, AOC, and QmP. All of these attempts to give order to a sea of wine don't ultimately guarantee a good wine. A vintner working on the cheap can make an uninteresting wine from a great vineyard and a dedicated winemaker can make stunning wine from a lowly site. So look to the wineries that consistently please you, your friends, and wine professionals whose opinion you value, for the best assurance of quality in the bottle.

If you'd like to learn more about specific regions, you can find very detailed information about local climates, soils, and wineries in *Sotheby's Wine Encyclopedia, Hugh Johnson's World Atlas of Wine* or The *Wine Bible*. (See our Resources list on page 50 for more details.)

On the following pages we've provided maps of the major wine-producing areas in the world and tables of the grapes most commonly grown in each region, along with some information to help you decipher the labels on wines from particular areas.

In the U.S. it's usually simple to know the main grape in a bottle of wine as it's typically featured on the label. However, in many regions of the world, especially Europe, it's not so easy. Many European labels identify the region, not the grapes. And you're supposed to know which grapes are most likely grown in that region, or whether local laws require that only certain grapes be used in their wines. The tables will help to uncover the information in many of your wine labels.

france

loire valle

bordeaux

Figuring out where a wine from France was produced can be somewhat of a challenge. A wine from Burgundy may not clearly say Burgundy, but instead the label might highlight a region (known as an AOC or *appellation d'origine contrôlée*) within Burgundy.

To help decipher some of the French labels, here's a guide to the regions you might find, and the starring grapes in those areas.

champagne

★ PARIS

alsace

burgundy

france

northern rhône

southern rhône

MARSEILLE

languedoc-roussillon

★ provence

FRANCE		region								
famous name	**starring grapes**	Alsace	Bordeaux	Burgundy	Champagne	Loire Valley	Languedoc-Roussillon	Rhône Valley	Provence
Bandol	**Mourvèdre**								●
Alsace	Riesling Gewürztraminer Pinot Blanc Pinot Gris	●							
Banyuls	**Grenache**						●		
Barsac	Sauvignon Blanc Sémillon		●						
Beaujolais	**Gamay**			●					
Chablis	Chardonnay			●					
Champagne	Chardonnay **Pinot Noir** **Pinot Meunier**				●				
Châteauneuf-du-Pape	**Grenache** **Syrah** **Mourvèdre** **Cinsault** **Carignane**							●	
Chinon	**Cabernet Franc**					●			
Condrieu	Viognier							●	
Corbières	**Grenache** **Syrah** **Mourvèdre** **Cinsault** **Carignane**						●		

FRANCE		region							
famous name	**starring grapes**	Alsace	Bordeaux	Burgundy	Champagne	Loire Valley	Languedoc-Roussillon	Rhône Valley	Provence
Côte Chalonnaise	**Pinot Noir**			●					
Côte de Beaune	**Pinot Noir** Chardonnay			●					
Côte de Nuits	**Pinot Noir**			●					
Côte Rôtie	**Syrah**							●	
Côtes du Rhône	**Grenache Syrah Mourvèdre Cinsault Carignane**							●	
Crozes-Hermitage	**Syrah**							●	
Entre-Deux-Mers	Sauvignon Blanc Sémillon		●						
Gevrey-Chambertin	**Pinot Noir**			●					
Gigondas	**Grenache Syrah Mourvèdre**							●	
Givry	**Pinot Noir**			●					
Graves	**Cabernet Sauvignon Cabernet Franc Merlot** Sauvignon Blanc Sémillon		●						
Haut-Médoc and Médoc	**Cabernet Sauvignon Cabernet Franc Merlot**		●						

continued - - - - - - - - - - - ➜

FRANCE

famous name	starring grapes	Alsace	Bordeaux	Burgundy	Champagne	Loire Valley	Languedoc-Roussillon	Rhône Valley	Provence
Hermitage	**Syrah** Marsanne and Roussanne							●	
Mâcon	Chardonnay			●					
Margaux	**Cabernet Sauvignon** **Cabernet Franc** **Merlot**		●						
Meursault	Chardonnay			●					
Minervois	**Grenache** **Syrah** **Mourvèdre** **Carignane**						●		
Montrachet	Chardonnay			●					
Muscadet	Melon					●			
Pauillac	**Cabernet Sauvignon** **Cabernet Franc** **Merlot**		●						
Pessac-Léognan	**Cabernet Sauvignon** **Cabernet Franc** **Merlot** Sauvignon Blanc Sémillon		●						
Pomerol	**Merlot** **Cabernet Sauvignon** **Cabernet Franc**		●						

FRANCE		region								
famous name	**starring grapes**	Alsace	Bordeaux	Burgundy	Champagne	Loire Valley	Languedoc-Roussillon	Rhône Valley	Provence	
Pommard	**Pinot Noir**			●						
Pouilly-Fuissé	Chardonnay			●						
Pouilly-Fumé	Sauvignon Blanc					●				
Saint-Émilion	**Merlot** **Cabernet Franc** **Cabernet Sauvignon**		●							
Saint-Estèphe	**Cabernet Sauvignon** **Cabernet Franc** **Merlot** **Malbec** **Petit Verdot**		●							
Saint-Julien	**Cabernet Sauvignon** **Cabernet Franc** **Merlot**		●							
Sancerre	Sauvignon Blanc					●				
Sauternes	Sauvignon Blanc Sémillon		●							
Tavel	Rosé only—primarily from **Grenache**							●		
Volnay	**Pinot Noir**			●						
Vosne-Romanée	**Pinot Noir**			●						
Vouvray	Chenin Blanc					●				

piedmont

ven
VENICE

FLOREN
tuscar

italy

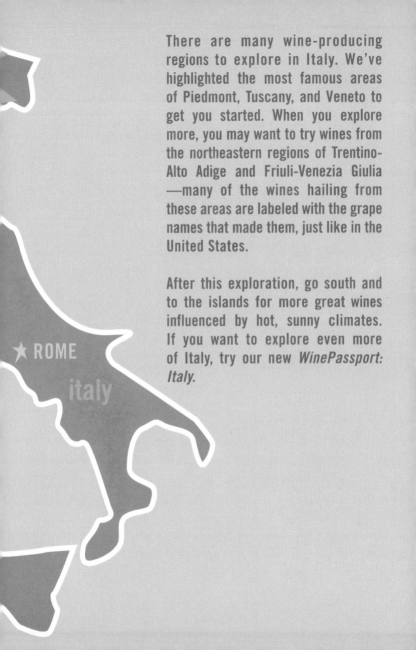

There are many wine-producing regions to explore in Italy. We've highlighted the most famous areas of Piedmont, Tuscany, and Veneto to get you started. When you explore more, you may want to try wines from the northeastern regions of Trentino-Alto Adige and Friuli-Venezia Giulia —many of the wines hailing from these areas are labeled with the grape names that made them, just like in the United States.

After this exploration, go south and to the islands for more great wines influenced by hot, sunny climates. If you want to explore even more of Italy, try our new *WinePassport: Italy*.

★ ROME

italy

ITALY

famous name	starring grapes	region		
		Tuscany	Piedmont	Veneto
Barbaresco	**Nebbiolo**		●	
Barbera d'Alba et alia	**Barbera**		●	
Barolo	**Nebbiolo**		●	
Bolgheri	**Cabernet Sauvignon** **Merlot**	●		
Brunello di Montalcino	**Brunello** (clone of Sangiovese)	●		
Carmignano	**Sangiovese** **Cabernet Sauvignon**	●		
Chianti Classico Chianti Rufina Chianti	**Sangiovese**	●		
Dolcetto d'Alba et alia	**Dolcetto**		●	
Gattinara	**Nebbiolo**		●	

ITALY

famous name	starring grapes	Tuscany	Piedmont	Veneto
Gavi	Cortese		●	
Moscato d'Asti	Muscat		●	
Prosecco	Prosecco			●
Roero Arneis	Arneis		●	
Soave	Garganega			●
Valpolicella Amarone Della Valpolicella Recioto Della Valpolicella	**Corvina**			●
Vernaccia di San Gimignano	Vernaccia	●		
Vin Santo	Malvasia Trebbiano	●		
Vino Nobile di Montepulciano	**Prugnolo (clone of Sangiovese)**	●		

While local red wine production is on the rise, Germany is best known for its white wines. Most German wine labels list the main grape used to make the wine. The most notable white grape varieties you'll find in German wines are Gerwürztraminer, Müller-Thurgau (a cross between Riesling and Chasselas), Riesling, Silvaner, Weissburgunder (Pinot Blanc), and Graubunger (Pinot Gris).

germany + austria

Like its neighbor Germany, Austria is best known for its white wines. The most notable ones to look for are: Grüner Veltliner, Welschriesling, Neuburger, Riesling and Muskateller, as well as Chardonnay and Pinot Gris (sometimes referred to as Ruländer or Grauer Burgunder). Austria also produces some interesting reds, including Blaufränkisch, St. Laurent, and Zweigelt.

COLOG
★

pfa

Don't ignore those Rieslings!

American wine drinkers often assume that Rieslings are sugary sweet. Whether you like sweet wine or not, you can probably find a Riesling that suits you. Many are in fact quite dry and they go great with all sorts of food. An added bonus is that prices for most German Rieslings remain low since American consumers write them off as sweet wine. So the best, most concentrated, flavor-packed Rieslings, dry or sweet, remain a great bargain. The terms on the next page will help you know whether or not you're buying a sweet German wine.

how **Sweet** it is

German labels give information on how ripe the grapes were when they were picked and how sweet the wine is. And, grapes at a range of ripeness can be made into sweet or dry wines. So if you like your wine on the drier side, look for the words Halb-Trocken, which means semi-dry, and Trocken, which means dry. If you like dessert wines, you're likely to be romanced by the many levels of sweetness that German dessert wines offer:

BEERENAUSLESE
noticeably sweet wine

TROCKENBEERENAUSLESE
extremely sweet and syrupy

EISWEIN
This is a sweet dessert wine made from grapes that have frozen on the vine, which makes them very concentrated and sweet.

Other words you may see on a German label include Kabinett, which generally refers to a light wine that can range from dry to slightly sweet, and Spätlese, which refers to a late harvest wine, where the grapes are picked at least seven days after the main harvest. These wines can range from dry to sweet as well.

As in Italy, there are many great wine-producing regions to explore in Spain and Portugal. These wine industries are evolving rapidly, and bargains abound. More of these wines are making their way to the United States, and we've highlighted a few of the regions that you'll likely see in your local wine shop.

If you're trying some of the sparkling wines from Spain (known as Cava), you may see the region Penedès on the label, as this area is known for Cava. However, many other regions in Spain produce sparkling wines as well.

spain + portugal

rías baix

★POR
porto
e dour

★LISBON
portugal

madeira

rioja & navarra

ribera del duero

penedès

MADRID

priorato

spain

SEVILLE

jerez

Port + Sherry

Portugal and Spain have given us two delicious wines, port and sherry. Both wines are fortified, meaning they have had alcohol (grape spirits) added to them.

The name port, or 'porto', comes from the Portuguese town Porto in northern Portugal, where much of the nation's port was shipped from. With port, alcohol is added *during* fermentation, which stops the fermenting process, so some of the sugars in the wine have not converted to alcohol. This is why port can be quite sweet.

The word sherry comes from Jerez, a southern Spanish town where much of Spain's top sherry is made. In sherry the alcohol is added *after* fermentation, so the wines tend to be dry (though there can be sweet sherries too). Another unique feature of sherry is the Solera System, which is an aging process where winemakers mix vintages to give a consistent taste from year to year, and let air into the barrels as the wine ages (giving it an oxidized, or sometimes nutty taste).

There are many types of ports and sherries, offering a wonderful range of flavors and colors—explore them and see which you like best.

SPAIN+PORTUGAL		region		
famous name	**starring grapes**	Northern Spain	Southern Spain	Portugal
Madeira	Sercial Verdelho Bual (Boal) Malmsey (Malvasia)			●
Navarra	**Garnacha** **Tempranillo** **Cabernet Sauvignon** **Merlot**	●		
Penedès (known for its Cava)	Macabeo Xarel-lo Parellada Chardonnay **Cariñena** **Garnacha** **Monastrell** **Cabernet Sauvignon**	●		
Porto/Port (Tawny or Ruby) Douro (Table Wine)	**Touriga Nacional** **Tinto Cão** **Tinta Roriz** **Tinta Barroca** **Touriga Francesa**			●
Rías Baixas	**Albariño**	●		
Ribera del Duero	**Tempranillo** (aka Tinto Fino or Tinto del País) **Cabernet Sauvignon** **Merlot**	●		
Rioja	**Tempranillo** **Garnacha**	●		
Sherry (or Jerez)	Palomino Pedro Ximénez Moscatel (Muscat)		●	

california

mendocino
sierra foothills
lodi

SACRAMENTO

sonoma — **napa** ★

★ SAN FRANCISCO

san joaquin

california

santa cruz mountains

— **paso robles**
★ SAN LUIS OBISPO
— **edna valley**
— **santa maria valley**
— **santa ynez valley**
★ SANTA BARBARA
★ LOS ANGELES
★ SAN DIEGO

Since there are no laws about which grapes may be used in American wines, you'll find a wide range of grapes, from the common to the obscure, grown in all parts of the country. Yet there are U.S. labeling rules, and understanding these can prove quite useful. While certainly not necessary, you may want to learn them, if only for bragging rights at your next cocktail party.

washington

★ SEATTLE

columbia valley

yakima valley

walla walla
valley

washington + oregon

columbia valley

walla walla
valley

★

PORTLAND

willamette valley

umpqua valley

oregon

rogue valley

If you see this on the label:	The wine contains this percent of grapes:	Meaning:
Specific Grape (such as Pinot Grigio, Chardonnay)	**75%**	At least 75% of the wine is made from that grape. While some wine-makers may list the other grapes used to make the wines, they're not required.
A Country or an American County or State	**75%**	At least 75% of the grapes must come from that county, state or country.
Region or AVA (such as Central Coast or Russian River)	**85%**	85% of the grapes were grown in that area.
Vineyard	**95%**	95% of the wine must have been grown on the vineyard itself.

If you see this on the label:	The wine contains this percent of grapes:	Meaning:
Vintage Date	**95%**	At least 95% of the grapes must have been harvested in that year. *Note: Sparkling wines are often blends from several vintages, labeled as N.V. or Non-Vintage. This does not mean the wine is inferior.*
Estate Bottled	**100%**	The winery grew or directed the growing of the grapes, all of which must come from the winery's AVA. *Note: the words "Estate Bottled" do not guarantee better wine.*
Reserve		Many winemakers will label their highest quality wine "reserve." Although it sounds elegant, it has no legal requirements attached to it.

Chile has become well-known for reasonably priced, quality wines, especially Cabernet Sauvignon and Merlot, and Chardonnay and Sauvignon Blanc.

chile + argentina

And Argentina similarly is producing reasonably priced wines from several grape varieties, including Cabernet Sauvignon, Merlot, Syrah, and Barbera. Argentina's claim to fame is wine made from Malbec grapes, which in most other countries is generally blended with other grapes rather than used on its own.

chile
argentina
BUENOS
AIRES
casablanca
SANTIAGO
mendoza
maipo
curicó
rio negro

australia

australia

Like their American counterparts, Austrialian winemakers a
permitted to grow any grape they like in any region. Some of the mo
popular grapes from down under include Australian Shiraz (Syra
Cabernet Sauvignon, Merlot, Chardonnay, and Riesling, and frequent
blends of these wines. They also feature some lesser-known grap
such as Chambourcin and Verdelho. Finally, Aussie winemakers a
embracing sparkling Shiraz and other red sparklings that a
certainly worth tracking down.

New Zealand is also becoming a major player in the international wi
world. It's home to many well-known wineries and while it produc
many lovely reds, it is best known for its Sauvignon Blancs a
Chardonnays.

South African wines are still emerging in the U.S. and wine drinkers are beginning to explore their offerings even more. South Africa's largest production is white wine, much of it Chenin Blanc, also known as Steen in South Africa. The main regions are in the south, at the Cape: Constantia, Stellenbosch, Franschhoek, and Paarl. The most common grape varieties you'll see coming out of South Africa include: Steen (Chenin Blanc), Sauvignon Blanc, Chardonnay, Cabernet Sauvignon, Merlot, Cinsault, and Pinotage (a cross between Pinot Noir and Cinsault).

south africa

DURBANVILLE

CAPETOWN

south africa

paarl

franschhoek

stellenbosch

nstantia

thirsty for
More?

We hope WineNotes has sparked your thirst for more wine knowledge. If so, check out our WineSmarts question and answer cards, WineParty winetasting kit, and WinePassport guides to Italy and California. Visit **www.smartsco.com** for alist of retailers.

There are also hundreds of great print and online resources that can teach you more. Here are just a few that we've found both useful and friendly.

Fear of Wine – An Introductory Guide to the Grape
Leslie Brenner, illustrated by Lettie Teague (Bantam Books, 1995).

Great Wine Made Simple
Andrea Immer (Broadway Books, a division of Random House, 2000).

New Sotheby's Wine Encyclopedia
Tom Stevenson (DK Publishing, 2001).

The Oxford Companion to Wine
Edited by Jancis Robinson (Oxford University Press, 1999).

Windows on the World Complete Wine Course
Kevin Zraly (Sterling Publishing Company, 2003).

The Wine Bible
Karen MacNeil (Workman Publishing Company, 2001).

The New Wine Lover's Companion – Comprehensive Definitions for More than 3500 Wine-Related Terms
Ron Herbst and Sharon Tyler Herbst (Barron's, 2nd Edition, 2003).

The World Atlas of Wine
Hugh Johnson and Jancis Robinson (Mitchell Beazley, 2001).

Of course, the best way to refine your palate is to taste wine, and taste lots of it. Taste it with and without food. Taste it with other people so you can talk about it. Because, like wine, knowledge is meant to be shared. Enjoy!

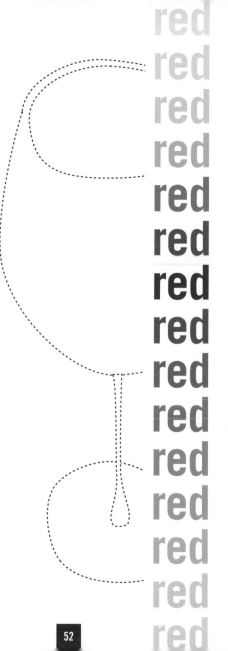

red
red
red
red
red
red
red
red
red
red
red
red
red
red

winery _____ vintage _____

region _____

grape(s) _____

color/aroma _____

taste _____

overall opinion _____

_____ price

$

winery _____ vintage _____

region _____

grape(s) _____

color/aroma _____

taste _____

overall opinion _____

_____ price

$

winery _____ vintage _____

region _____

grape(s) _____

color/aroma _____

taste _____

overall opinion _____

_____ price

$

q True or False: Zinfandel is the name of a blend of grapes.

winery _____ vintage _____

region _____

grape(s) _____

color/aroma _____

taste _____

overall opinion _____

_____ price

$

winery _____ vintage _____

region _____

grape(s) _____

color/aroma _____

taste _____

overall opinion _____

price

$ _____

False. It's a grape type mainly grown in California. a

winery _____ vintage _____

region _____

grape(s) _____

color/aroma _____

taste _____

overall opinion _____

price

$ _____

winery _____ vintage _____

region _____

grape(s) _____

color/aroma _____

taste _____

overall opinion _____

_____ price

$

q Beaujolais wines are made from which grape?

winery _____ vintage _____

region _____

grape(s) _____

color/aroma _____

taste _____

overall opinion _____

_____ price

$

winery _____ vintage _____

region _____

grape(s) _____

color/aroma _____

taste _____

overall opinion _____

_____ price

$ ____

Gamay.

winery _____ vintage _____

region _____

grape(s) _____

color/aroma _____

taste _____

overall opinion _____

price

$ ____

winery _____ vintage _____

region _____

grape(s) _____

color/aroma _____

taste _____

overall opinion _____

_____ price

$

q True or False: Shiraz and Syrah are the same grape.

winery _____ vintage _____

region _____

grape(s) _____

color/aroma _____

taste _____

overall opinion _____

_____ price

$

winery _____   vintage _____

region _____

grape(s) _____

color/aroma _____

taste _____

overall opinion _____

_____   price

$

True. **a**

winery _____   vintage _____

region _____

grape(s) _____

color/aroma _____

taste _____

overall opinion _____

_____   price

$

winery _____ vintage _____

region _____

grape(s) _____

color/aroma _____

taste _____

overall opinion _____

price

$

q True or False: Syrah and Petite Sirah are the same grape.

winery _____ vintage _____

region _____

grape(s) _____

color/aroma _____

taste _____

overall opinion _____

price

$

winery _____ vintage _____

region _____

grape(s) _____

color/aroma _____

taste _____

overall opinion _____

_____ price

$

False. a

winery _____ vintage _____

region _____

grape(s) _____

color/aroma _____

taste _____

overall opinion _____

_____ price

$

winery _____ vintage _____

region _____

grape(s) _____

color/aroma _____

taste _____

overall opinion _____

_____ price

$

q Barbaresco wines are made from which type of grape?

winery _____ vintage _____

region _____

grape(s) _____

color/aroma _____

taste _____

overall opinion _____

_____ price

$

winery _____ vintage _____

region _____

grape(s) _____

color/aroma _____

taste _____

overall opinion _____

_____ price

$

Nebbiolo. **a**

winery _____ vintage _____

region _____

grape(s) _____

color/aroma _____

taste _____

overall opinion _____

_____ price

$

red notes

winery _____ vintage _____

region _____

grape(s) _____

color/aroma _____

taste _____

overall opinion _____

price
_____ $

q What is the primary grape used in Chianti?

winery _____ vintage _____

region _____

grape(s) _____

color/aroma _____

taste _____

overall opinion _____

price
_____ $

winery _____ vintage _____

region _____

grape(s) _____

color/aroma _____

taste _____

overall opinion _____

_____ price

$

Sangiovese.

winery _____ vintage _____

region _____

grape(s) _____

color/aroma _____

taste _____

overall opinion _____

_____ price

$

winery _____ vintage _____

region _____

grape(s) _____

color/aroma _____

taste _____

overall opinion _____

price

_____ $

q **What is the top classification of Burgundy wines?**

winery _____ vintage _____

region _____

grape(s) _____

color/aroma _____

taste _____

overall opinion _____

price

_____ $

winery _____ vintage _____

region _____

grape(s) _____

color/aroma _____

taste _____

overall opinion _____

_____ price

$

Grand Cru.

winery _____ vintage _____

region _____

grape(s) _____

color/aroma _____

taste _____

overall opinion _____

_____ price

$

winery _____ vintage _____

region _____

grape(s) _____

color/aroma _____

taste _____

overall opinion _____

_____ price

$

q **What is the top classification of Bordeaux wines?**

winery _____ vintage _____

region _____

grape(s) _____

color/aroma _____

taste _____

overall opinion _____

_____ price

$

winery _____ vintage _____

region _____

grape(s) _____

color/aroma _____

taste _____

overall opinion _____

_____ price

$

Premier Cru.

winery _____ vintage _____

region _____

grape(s) _____

color/aroma _____

taste _____

overall opinion _____

_____ price

$

winery _____ vintage _____

region _____

grape(s) _____

color/aroma _____

taste _____

overall opinion _____

price

_____ $

q   **Maipo Valley is a region in which country?**

winery _____ vintage _____

region _____

grape(s) _____

color/aroma _____

taste _____

overall opinion _____

price

_____ $

winery _____ vintage _____

region _____

grape(s) _____

color/aroma _____

taste _____

overall opinion _____

_____ price

$

Chile. **a**

winery _____ vintage _____

region _____

grape(s) _____

color/aroma _____

taste _____

overall opinion _____

_____ price

$

winery _____ vintage _____

region _____

grape(s) _____

color/aroma _____

taste _____

overall opinion _____

_____ price

$

True or False: Chianti wines come from Tuscany.

winery _____ vintage _____

region _____

grape(s) _____

color/aroma _____

taste _____

overall opinion _____

_____ price

$

winery _____ vintage _____

region _____

grape(s) _____

color/aroma _____

taste _____

overall opinion _____

_____ price

$

True. **a**

winery _____ vintage _____

region _____

grape(s) _____

color/aroma _____

taste _____

overall opinion _____

price

$

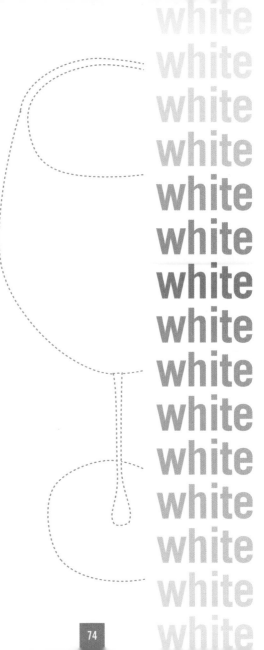

white
white
white
white
white
white
white
white
white
white
white
white
white
white
white

winery _____ vintage _____

region _____

grape(s) _____

color/aroma _____

taste _____

overall opinion _____

_____ price

$

winery _____ vintage _____

region _____

grape(s) _____

color/aroma _____

taste _____

overall opinion _____

_____ price

$

winery _____ vintage _____

region _____

grape(s) _____

color/aroma _____

taste _____

overall opinion _____

_____ price

$

q **White Hermitage is made from what grapes?**

winery _____ vintage _____

region _____

grape(s) _____

color/aroma _____

taste _____

overall opinion _____

_____ price

$

winery _____ vintage _____

region _____

grape(s) _____

color/aroma _____

taste _____

overall opinion _____

price

$

Marsanne and Roussanne.

winery _____ vintage _____

region _____

grape(s) _____

color/aroma _____

taste _____

overall opinion _____

price

$

winery _____ vintage _____

region _____

grape(s) _____

color/aroma _____

taste _____

overall opinion _____

price
_____ $

q **True or False: Trebbiano is a white wine-producing grape.**

winery _____ vintage _____

region _____

grape(s) _____

color/aroma _____

taste _____

overall opinion _____

price
_____ $

winery _____ vintage _____

region _____

grape(s) _____

color/aroma _____

taste _____

overall opinion _____

price

_____ $

True. *a*

winery _____ vintage _____

region _____

grape(s) _____

color/aroma _____

taste _____

overall opinion _____

price

_____ $

winery _____ vintage _____

region _____

grape(s) _____

color/aroma _____

taste _____

overall opinion _____

_____ price

$

q **French Chablis is made from which grape?**

winery _____ vintage _____

region _____

grape(s) _____

color/aroma _____

taste _____

overall opinion _____

_____ price

$

winery _____ vintage _____

region _____

grape(s) _____

color/aroma _____

taste _____

overall opinion _____

_____ price

$

Chardonnay, as with nearly all other whites from Burgundy. a

winery _____ vintage _____

region _____

grape(s) _____

color/aroma _____

taste _____

overall opinion _____

_____ price

$

winery _____ vintage _____

region _____

grape(s) _____

color/aroma _____

taste _____

overall opinion _____

_____ price

$

q **What is the most widely planted grape in New Zealand?**

winery _____ vintage _____

region _____

grape(s) _____

color/aroma _____

taste _____

overall opinion _____

_____ price

$

winery _____ vintage _____

region _____

grape(s) _____

color/aroma _____

taste _____

overall opinion _____

_____ price

$

Chardonnay. a

winery _____ vintage _____

region _____

grape(s) _____

color/aroma _____

taste _____

overall opinion _____

_____ price

$

winery _____ vintage _____

region _____

grape(s) _____

color/aroma _____

taste _____

overall opinion _____

price

$

q **What is Condrieu?**

winery _____ vintage _____

region _____

grape(s) _____

color/aroma _____

taste _____

overall opinion _____

price

$

winery _____ vintage _____

region _____

grape(s) _____

color/aroma _____

taste _____

overall opinion _____

price
_____ $

A white wine from the northern Rhône. *a*

winery _____ vintage _____

region _____

grape(s) _____

color/aroma _____

taste _____

overall opinion _____

price
_____ $

winery _____ vintage _____

region _____

grape(s) _____

color/aroma _____

taste _____

overall opinion _____

price
_____ $

q **Ture or False: Vinho Verde is a type of grape.**

winery _____ vintage _____

region _____

grape(s) _____

color/aroma _____

taste _____

overall opinion _____

price
_____ $

winery _____ vintage _____

region _____

grape(s) _____

color/aroma _____

taste _____

overall opinion _____

_____ price

$ ____

False. It's a wine producing region in Portugal. **a**

winery _____ vintage _____

region _____

grape(s) _____

color/aroma _____

taste _____

overall opinion _____

_____ price

$ ____

winery _____ vintage _____

region _____

grape(s) _____

color/aroma _____

taste _____

overall opinion _____

_____ price

$

9 **What is Sancerre?**

winery _____ vintage _____

region _____

grape(s) _____

color/aroma _____

taste _____

overall opinion _____

_____ price

$

winery _____ vintage _____

region _____

grape(s) _____

color/aroma _____

taste _____

overall opinion _____

price

$

An area in the Loire Valley of France, famous for its Sauvignon Blanc. **a**

winery _____ vintage _____

region _____

grape(s) _____

color/aroma _____

taste _____

overall opinion _____

price

$

winery _____ vintage _____

region _____

grape(s) _____

color/aroma _____

taste _____

overall opinion _____

price
_____ $

q   **True or False: Marsanne is a region in France.**

winery _____ vintage _____

region _____

grape(s) _____

color/aroma _____

taste _____

overall opinion _____

price
_____ $

winery _____ vintage _____

region _____

grape(s) _____

color/aroma _____

taste _____

overall opinion _____

price
_____ $

False. It's a white grape variety. a

winery _____ vintage _____

region _____

grape(s) _____

color/aroma _____

taste _____

overall opinion _____

price
_____ $

winery _____ vintage _____

region _____

grape(s) _____

color/aroma _____

taste _____

overall opinion _____

price
_____

$

q **True or False: Tavel is a rosé wine.**

winery _____ vintage _____

region _____

grape(s) _____

color/aroma _____

taste _____

overall opinion _____

price

$

winery _____ vintage _____

region _____

grape(s) _____

color/aroma _____

taste _____

overall opinion _____

price

$

True. Tavel is a wine and an area in the southern Rhône. a

winery _____ vintage _____

region _____

grape(s) _____

color/aroma _____

taste _____

overall opinion _____

price

$

winery _____ vintage _____

region _____

grape(s) _____

color/aroma _____

taste _____

overall opinion _____

price
_____ $

q   True or False: Sémillon is a white wine grape.

winery _____ vintage _____

region _____

grape(s) _____

color/aroma _____

taste _____

overall opinion _____

price
$

winery _____ vintage _____

region _____

grape(s) _____

color/aroma _____

taste _____

overall opinion _____

price
$

True. It's often mixed with Sauvignon Blanc in Bordeaux. a

winery _____ vintage _____

region _____

grape(s) _____

color/aroma _____

taste _____

overall opinion _____

price
$

sparkling
sparkling
sparkling
sparkling
sparkling
sparkling
sparkling
sparkling
sparkling
sparkling
sparkling
sparkling
sparkling
sparkling
sparkling

winery _____ vintage _____

region _____

grape(s) _____

color/aroma _____

taste _____

overall opinion _____

_____ price

$

winery _____ vintage _____

region _____

grape(s) _____

color/aroma _____

taste _____

overall opinion _____

_____ price

$

winery _____ vintage _____

region _____

grape(s) _____

color/aroma _____

taste _____

overall opinion _____

price

$

q **What type of grape is in a Blanc de Blancs champagne?**

winery _____ vintage _____

region _____

grape(s) _____

color/aroma _____

taste _____

overall opinion _____

price

$

winery _____ vintage _____

region _____

grape(s) _____

color/aroma _____

taste _____

overall opinion _____

price

_____ $

Chardonnay.

winery _____ vintage _____

region _____

grape(s) _____

color/aroma _____

taste _____

overall opinion _____

price

_____ $

winery _____ vintage _____

region _____

grape(s) _____

color/aroma _____

taste _____

overall opinion _____

price

_____

$

q What type of grape is in a Blanc de Noirs champagne?

winery _____ vintage _____

region _____

grape(s) _____

color/aroma _____

taste _____

overall opinion _____

price

_____

$

winery _____ vintage _____

region _____

grape(s) _____

color/aroma _____

taste _____

overall opinion _____

price

$

Pinot Noir and often Pinot Meunier. a

winery _____ vintage _____

region _____

grape(s) _____

color/aroma _____

taste _____

overall opinion _____

price

$

dessert
dessert
dessert
dessert
dessert
dessert
dessert
dessert
dessert
dessert
dessert
dessert
dessert
dessert
dessert

winery _____ vintage _____

region _____

grape(s) _____

color/aroma _____

taste _____

overall opinion _____

_____ price

$

winery _____ vintage _____

region _____

grape(s) _____

color/aroma _____

taste _____

overall opinion _____

_____ price

$

winery _____ vintage _____

region _____

grape(s) _____

color/aroma _____

taste _____

overall opinion _____

price
_____
$

q **Sauternes is usually made from which two grapes?**

winery _____ vintage _____

region _____

grape(s) _____

color/aroma _____

taste _____

overall opinion _____

price
_____
$

winery _____ vintage _____

region _____

grape(s) _____

color/aroma _____

taste _____

overall opinion _____

_____ price

$

Sémillon and Sauvignon Blanc.

winery _____ vintage _____

region _____

grape(s) _____

color/aroma _____

taste _____

overall opinion _____

_____ price

$

winery _____ vintage _____

region _____

grape(s) _____

color/aroma _____

taste _____

overall opinion _____

_____ price

$

q True or False: Muscat and Muscadet are two different types of grapes.

winery _____ vintage _____

region _____

grape(s) _____

color/aroma _____

taste _____

overall opinion _____

_____ price

$

winery _____ vintage _____

region _____

grape(s) _____

color/aroma _____

taste _____

overall opinion _____

price

_____ $

True. a

winery _____ vintage _____

region _____

grape(s) _____

color/aroma _____

taste _____

overall opinion _____

price

_____ $

Get a taste of
Other SmartsCo Titles

Visit our web site at www.smartsco.com for new ideas for winetasting parties, updates on wine events near you, and information on our other wine products. Here's just a taste of SmartsCo's other wine and food games and journals:

WineParty. For a great time, just add wine. This stylish winetasting kit makes it easy to explore wine with friends. Inside is everything you need to throw an entertaining and informative winetasting for four or thirty-four.

WinePassports: California, Italy, France, Bubbly, Portugal. Drink like a local. These friendly pocket guides with pop-out maps quickly make sense of wines, grapes, and regions. All so you can concentrate on enjoying new wine discoveries!

WineSmarts. It'll go straight to your head. Called "the greatest game ever" by star chef Mario Batali, WineSmarts is an elegantly designed box of one-hundred question and answer cards and WineTips guide that finally makes learning about wine easy and fun for novice and expert wine lovers.

ChocolateSmarts. Cultivate your craving. From cocoa trees to chocolate bars, ChocolateSmarts offers everything you ever wanted to know about this delightful treat. Do you know which cocoa beans are the highest quality? The best way to melt chocolate? Or who made the first chocolate bar? You will after indulging in a box of ChocolateSmarts.

FoodSmarts. Feed your mind. FoodSmarts offers food lovers a fun, engaging way to learn about tasty items that appear on even the most complicated menus. One hundred question and answer cards and FoodTips guide all cook up useful and interesting facts, from popcorn to pot au feu.

BeerSmarts. Tap your knowledge. BeerSmarts is the fun and informative question and answer game all about beer. Grab your friends, pick one of the 60 question and answer cards and find out: What's the difference between a lager and an ale? What makes beer skunky? What's the world's oldest beer?

To order more SmartsCo products, including our newest BeerSmarts and CoffeeSmarts visit www.smartsco.com.

Unless you speak French, German, Italian, and Spanish, you might find it difficult to pronounce some of the names of wines or the regions they hail from. Here's a quick pronunciation guide for some of the better-known terms you might come across during your wine journey.